SCHOLASTIC

Success With Reading Comprehension

New York • Toronto • London • Auckland • Sydney
Mexico City • New Delhi • Hong Kong • Buenos Aires

Teaching *Resources*

State Standards Correlations

To find out how this book helps you meet your state's standards, log on to **www.scholastic.com/ssw**

Written by Robin Wolfe
Cover design by Ka-Yeon Kim-Li
Interior illustrations by Susan Hendron
Interior design by Quack & Company

ISBN 978-0-545-20082-0

Introduction

Reading can be fun when high-interest stories are paired with puzzles, brain teasers, and fun activities. Parents and teachers alike will find this book a valuable teaching tool. The purpose of the book is to help students at the third grade level improve their reading comprehension skills. They will practice finding the main idea and details, making inferences, following directions, drawing conclusions, and sequencing. Third graders are also challenged to develop vocabulary, understand cause and effect, distinguish between fact and opinion, and learn about story elements. They are encouraged to try reading strategies that will help them become better readers. Take a look at the Table of Contents. Teaching these valuable reading skills to your third graders will be a rewarding experience. Remember to praise them for their efforts and successes!

Table of Contents

SQ3R

Do you know about SQ3R? It is a formula to help you understand what you read. It can be useful for any reading assignment. SQ3R is especially helpful when you are reading a textbook, like your social studies or science book. Each letter of the formula tells you what to do.

S = Survey

Survey means to look over the assignment. Look at the pictures. Look at the title and the headings, if there are any. Read the first sentence or two.

Q = Question

Question means to ask yourself, "What is this assignment about? What is the author trying to tell me?" Once you get an idea of what you are going to read, then you can read with a better understanding.

3R = Read, Recite, Review

1. Read the assignment, looking for the answers to the questions you had. Concentrate. Picture in your mind what the words are saying.

2. Recite in your mind, or write on paper, the main ideas of what you have just read. Write the main ideas in your own words.

3. Review what you have learned. Make notes to help you review.

Now you have a valuable study tool. Use it to help study for a test. Use it to help remember what you read. Use it to help understand important information.

Let's practice. Read the assignment on page 5. Use the SQ3R formula step by step.

The Invention of the Telephone

Alexander Graham Bell invented the telephone. He was a teacher of the deaf in Boston. At night, he worked on experiments using a telegraph. Once when the metal in the telegraph stuck, Bell's assistant plucked the metal to loosen it. Bell, who was in another room, heard the sound in his receiver. He understood that the vibrations of the metal had traveled down the electric current to the receiver. He continued to work on this idea.

March 10, 1876, was the first time Alexander Graham Bell successfully spoke words over a telephone line. He was about to test a new transmitter when he spilled some battery acid on his clothes. He cried out to his assistant who was in another room, "Mr. Watson, come here! I want to see you!" Watson heard every word clearly on the telephone and rushed into the room.

Bell demonstrated his invention to many people. Over time, more and more telephone lines were installed, and people began to use the invention in their homes and businesses.

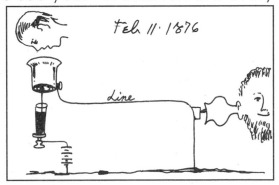

partial page from inventor's notebook

Did SQ3R help you? Let's find out.

1. Who invented the telephone? _____

2. What was his regular job? _____

3. What did Mr. Bell say to Mr. Watson during the first telephone conversation?

   _____

4. Who was Mr. Watson? _____

5. How did people first learn about the telephone? _____

   _____

On another sheet of paper, write a paragraph telling why you are glad the telephone was invented. Read your paragraph to a friend.

The Milky Way

The **main idea** of a story tells what the story is mostly about. **Details** in a story tell more information about the main idea.

What do you think of when you hear the words, "Milky Way"? Do you think of a candy bar? Well, there is another Milky Way, and you live in it! It is our galaxy. A galaxy is a grouping of stars. Scientists have learned that there are many galaxies in outer space. The Milky Way is a spiral-shaped galaxy with swirls of stars spinning out from the center of it. Some scientists believe there are hundreds of billions of stars in the Milky Way. One of those stars is the sun. Several planets orbit the sun. One of them is Earth. Even from Earth, on a clear night away from city lights, you can see part of the Milky Way. It is called that because so many stars close together look like a milky white stripe across the sky. However, if you looked at it with a telescope, you would see that it is made up of thousands of stars.

Complete the main idea and each detail about the story.

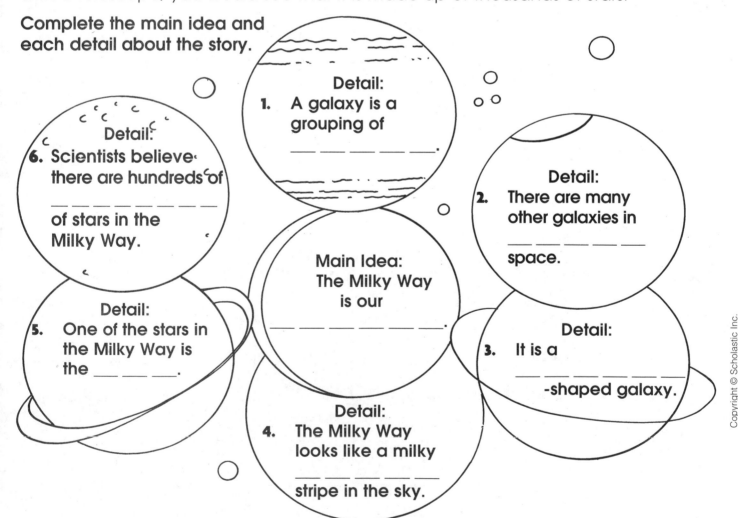

Detail:
1. A galaxy is a grouping of _____ _____ _____ _____.

Detail:
6. Scientists believe there are hundreds of _____ _____ _____ _____ of stars in the Milky Way.

Detail:
2. There are many other galaxies in _____ _____ _____ space.

Main Idea:
The Milky Way is our _____ _____ _____ _____.

Detail:
5. One of the stars in the Milky Way is the _____ _____ _____.

Detail:
3. It is a _____ _____ _____ _____ _____ -shaped galaxy.

Detail:
4. The Milky Way looks like a milky _____ _____ _____ _____ stripe in the sky.

Wagon Train

Will and Kate thought it would be a great adventure to travel west with the wagon train. In the spring of 1880, their family left their home in Pennsylvania and joined a wagon train headed for California. For months, their only home was the wagon. A large canvas was spread over metal hoops on top of the wagon to make a roof. Will helped his father oil the canvas so that the rain would slide off and keep them dry inside. Each day Kate and Will gathered wood as they walked beside the wagon. In the evening when the wagons stopped, Kate and her mother built a campfire for cooking supper. They hauled supplies with them so that they could cook beans and biscuits. Sometimes the men went hunting and brought back fresh deer meat or a rabbit for stew. When it rained for several days, the roads were so muddy that the wagons got stuck. There was always danger of snakes and bad weather. There were rivers and mountains to cross. There was no doctor to take care of those who got sick or injured. Will and Kate were right. Traveling with a wagon train was a great adventure, but it was a very hard life.

Unscramble the words to make a complete sentence that tells the main idea.

wagon dangerous. on a Life hard and was train _____

_____

Choose a word from the wagon to complete each detail.

1. __ __ __ __ __ __ the canvas

2. __ __ __ __ __ __ __ __ wood

3. __ __ __ __ __ __ __ over a campfire

4. __ __ __ __ __ __ __ supplies

5. __ __ __ __ __ __ __ for meat

6. __ __ __ __ __ __ __ __ out for snakes

7. __ __ __ __ __ __ __ for the rain to stop

8. __ __ __ __ __ __ __ __ __ rivers and mountains

9. __ __ __ __ __ __ __ __ sick or hurt with no doctor to help

getting   gathering   hunting
oiling   waiting   hauling
crossing   cooking   watching

What a Nose!

An elephant's trunk is probably the most useful nose in the world. Of course, it is used for breathing and smelling, like most noses are. However, elephants also use their trunks like arms and hands to lift food to their mouths. They suck water into their trunks and pour it into their mouths to get a drink. Sometimes they spray the water on their backs to give themselves a cool shower. An adult elephant can hold up to four gallons of water in its trunk. Elephants can use their trunks to carry heavy things, such as logs that weigh up to 600 pounds! The tip of the trunk has a little knob on it that the elephant uses like a thumb. An elephant can use the "thumb" to pick up something as small as a coin. Trunks are also used for communication. Two elephants that meet each other touch their trunks to each other's mouth, kind of like a kiss. Sometimes a mother elephant will calm her baby by stroking it with her trunk. Can your nose do all those things?

Find the statement below that is the main idea of the story. Write _M.I._ in the elephant next to it. Then find the details of the story. Write _D_ in the elephant next to each detail. Be careful! There are two sentences that do not belong in this story.

 Elephants use their trunks to greet each other, like giving a kiss.

 Elephants use their trunks to give themselves a shower.

 Some people like to ride on elephants.

 Elephants can carry heavy things with their trunks.

 Mother elephants calm their babies by stroking them with their trunks.

 Elephants use their trunks to eat and drink.

 Elephants use their noses for smelling and breathing.

 Elephants have very useful noses.

 Giraffes are the tallest animals in the world.

 On another sheet of paper, finish this story: When I was on safari, I looked up and saw a herd of elephants. Underline the main idea.

The Math Contest

Story elements *are the different parts of a story. The* **characters** *are the people, animals, or animated objects in the story. The* **setting** *is the place and time in which the story takes place. The* **plot** *of the story includes the events and often includes a* **problem** *and a* **solution**.

Every Friday, Mr. Jefferson, the math teacher, held a contest for his students. Sometimes they played math baseball. Sometimes they had math relays with flash cards. Other times, they were handed a sheet of paper with a hundred multiplication problems on it. The student who finished fastest with the most correct answers won the contest. One Friday, there was a math bee. It was similar to a spelling bee, except the students worked math problems in their heads. There was fierce competition, until finally, everyone was out of the game except Riley and Rhonda. Mr. Jefferson challenged them with problem after problem, but both students continued to answer correctly every time. It was almost time for class to end, so Mr. Jefferson gave them the same difficult problem. They had to work it in their heads. Riley thought hard and answered, "20." Rhonda answered, "18." Finally they had a winner!

7	4	6	5	3	1	2	6	4	8	0
6	9	1	4	3	5	6	2	8	6	7
5	0	8	6	0	4	9	7	3	1	4
3	1	7	4	0	6	5	8	7	2	6
7	0	6	5	8	4	9	3	2	9	6
8	4	9	8	0	6	1	5	7	8	4
6	2	7	3	9	2	4	8	1	6	5
6	4	4	6	1	9	0	6	6	2	3

To find out who won the game, work the problem below in your head. Write the answer on the blank.

$$6 + 4 + 6 - 4 - 4 + 6 + 6 = \underline{\qquad}$$

Now, to see if you are correct, circle only the 6's and 4's in the box. The answer will appear.

Answer each question below.

1. Name the three people in the story. _____, _____, and _____

2. Circle where the story takes place.
   a. in the gym   b. in the cafeteria   c. in Mr. Jefferson's classroom

3. Circle the problem in the story.
   a. Mr. Jefferson held the contest on Thursday.
   b. Class was almost over, and the contest was still tied.
   c. Riley and Rhonda both answered incorrectly.

4. Who answered the difficult question correctly? _____

Name _____

Best Friends

Amy dreaded recess every day. She did not have any friends to play with. All the girls in her class were paired up with a best friend or in groups, and she always felt left out. So, instead of playing with anyone, Amy just walked around by herself. She wanted to seesaw, but that is something you need to do with a friend. She liked to swing, but she could not go very high. She wished someone would push her to get her started.

One day, the teacher, Mrs. Gibbs, walked up and put her arm around Amy. "What's the matter, Amy? Why don't you play with the other children?" she asked kindly.

Amy replied, "Everyone has a friend except me. I don't have anyone." Mrs. Gibbs smiled and said, "Amy, the way to get a friend is to be a friend." Amy asked, "How do I do that?"

Mrs. Gibbs answered, "Look around the playground. There are three classes of third-graders out here during this recess time. Find someone who is alone and needs a friend. Then go to that person and ask them to play." Amy said she would think about it, but she was afraid she would be too embarrassed. She wasn't sure she could do it.

The next day, Amy noticed a dark-haired girl all alone on the playground. She worked up her courage and walked over to the girl. "Hi! My name is Amy. Do you want to play with me?" she asked.

"Okay," the girl said shyly. As they took turns pushing each other on the swings, Amy found out that the girl's name was Ming. She and her family had just moved from Japan. She did not know anyone and could not speak much English yet. She needed a friend.

"Want to seesaw?" Amy asked. Ming looked puzzled. Amy pointed to the seesaw. Ming smiled and nodded. Amy was so happy. She finally had a friend!

Name _____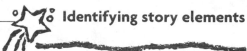

On each blank, write the letter of the picture that correctly answers the question.
One answer is used twice.

1. Where does this story take place? _____

2. Who is the main character in the story? _____

   Who are the other two characters in the story? _____ and _____

3. What is the problem in the story? _____

4. How does Amy solve her problem? _____

5. What is Ming's problem? _____

   How does Ming's problem get solved? _____

A. Mrs. Gibbs

B. playground

C. Ming needed a friend, too.

D. Ming

E. Amy

F. Amy asked Ming to play, and they became friends.

G. Amy needed a friend.

 Think about what you did during recess or another part of your day. On another sheet of paper, list the characters, setting, problem, and solution. Use this list to write a story. Read the story to a friend.

Name _____

The Tallest Trees

Redwood trees are the tallest trees in the world. Some grow over 300 feet high, which is taller than a 30-story building. Think of it this way: If a six-foot tall man stood at the base of a redwood tree, the tree would be 50 times taller than the man! These giant trees grow near the **coast** of California and Oregon. The **climate** is foggy and rainy there, which gives the redwoods a **constant** supply of water. Redwoods can grow for hundreds of years; in fact, some have lived for over 2,000 years! The **bark** is very thick, protecting the trees from insects, **disease**, and fires. The bark of redwood trees is a reddish-brown color. Redwood trees are very important to the lumber companies because the trees are so large that each one can be cut into lots of **lumber**. You may have seen lumber like this in redwood fences or redwood patio furniture. However, many of the trees are protected by law in the Redwood National Park. Lumber companies cannot cut trees that grow there. This is so the trees will not become **extinct**.

Put an X beside the correct definition of each bolded word in the story.

1. coast   ____ land by the sea   ____ a desert
2. climate   ____ time   ____ weather
3. constant   ____ happens regularly   ____ never happens
4. bark   ____ leaves   ____ outer covering of trees
5. disease   ____ illness   ____ high temperatures
6. lumber   ____ plastic pipes   ____ wood cut into boards
7. extinct   ____ no longer existing   ____ expensive

Read an article about another type of tree. On another sheet of paper, list five new words from the article. Use a dictionary to learn the meaning of each word.

Let's Play Soccer!

Soccer is the world's most popular sport. It is played in many countries all over the world. Every four years, an international competition is held. It is called the World Cup.

A **soccer field** is rectangular with a goal on each end. Each **goal** is made of a rectangular, net-covered frame. The game is played with a **soccer ball**. The ball is usually made of leather and is filled with air.

Two teams compete against each other. One point is awarded to a team when it scores a goal. Whichever team scores the most goals wins the game.

There are 11 players on each team. **Forwards** have the most responsibility to score goals. Sometimes forwards are called strikers. They are helped by teammates who play at midfield. These players are sometimes called **halfbacks**. Halfbacks help to score goals and try to keep the other team's ball away from the goal. Other teammates play farther back on the field to defend their goal. They try to keep the other team from getting close enough to score. They are sometimes called **fullbacks**. Each team has one **goalie** whose job is to keep the other team from scoring by blocking the ball or catching it before it goes into the goal. A goalie may catch or throw the ball, but no other players may use their hands. They may use their feet, legs, chest, or head to move the ball. A **referee** will penalize a team if any players other than the goalie use their hands. Soccer is definitely a team sport. All the positions are important in winning the game.

Label the diagram using the bolded words from the story.

Scrambled Eggs

 Sequencing *means putting the events of a story in the order in which they happened.*

The sentences below are scrambled. Number them in the correct sequence.

A. ____ I took a shower.
____ I got out of bed.
____ I got dressed.

B. ____ She planted the seeds.
____ Big pink flowers bloomed.
____ Tiny green shoots came up.

C. ____ He ate the sandwich.
____ He spread some jelly on them.
____ He got out two pieces of bread.

D. ____ He slid down the slide.
____ He climbed up the ladder.
____ He landed on his feet.

E. ____ We built a snowman.
____ Low gray clouds drifted in.
____ It began to snow hard.

F. ____ Firefighters put out the fire.
____ Lightning struck the barn.
____ The barn caught on fire.

G. ____ The pepper spilled out of the jar.
____ I sneezed.
____ My nose began to itch.

H. ____ "My name is Emma."
____ "Hi, what is your name?"
____ "It's nice to meet you, Emma."

I. ____ I said, "Okay, do a trick first."
____ Rover whined for a treat.
____ I gave him a dog biscuit.
____ He danced on his hind legs.

J. ____ She built a nest.
____ Baby birds hatched from the eggs.
____ I saw a robin gathering straw.
____ She laid four blue eggs.

My Crazy Dream

I don't know why, but I went to school in my underwear. Everyone was laughing! I walked up and down the hall looking for my classroom, but I could never find it. Then I went to the Lost and Found box and put on some clothes. I heard my principal say, "Son, are you lost?" However, when I turned around, it was the President of the United States talking to me. He asked me to fly on his jet with him. As we were flying, I looked out the window and saw a pterodactyl flying next to us! How could that be? They are extinct! It smiled and waved good-bye. Then all of a sudden, the airplane turned into a roller coaster. It climbed upward a million miles, then down we went! For hours and hours we just kept going straight down! The roller coaster finally came to a stop, and I was on an island made entirely of chocolate. I ate a whole tree made of fudge! Then someone sneaked up behind me and captured me. He put me in a pot of boiling water to make soup out of me. I got hotter and hotter and hotter! Finally, I woke up and realized I had fallen asleep with my electric blanket on high.

Number the pictures in the order that they happened in the dream.

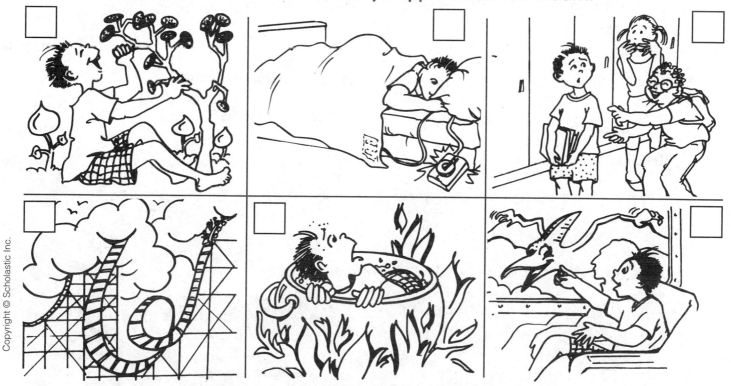

On another sheet of paper, draw a picture of a dream you once had. Then write a sentence about the beginning, middle, and end of the dream on separate strips of paper. Have a friend put the sentences in order.

Berry Colorful Ink

 When sequencing a story, look for key words such as first, then, next, *and* finally *to help you determine the correct sequence.*

In early American schools, students used a quill pen and ink to practice writing letters and numerals. Since these schools did not have many supplies, the students often had to make their own ink at home. There were many different ways to make ink. One of the most common ways was to use berries such as blackberries, blueberries, cherries, elderberries, or strawberries. The type of berry used depended on the color of ink a student wanted. First, the type of berry to be used had to gathered. Then a strainer was filled with the berries and held over a bowl. Next, using the back of a wooden spoon, the berries were crushed. This caused the juice to strain into the bowl. After all the berry juice was strained into the bowl, salt and vinegar were added to the juice and then stirred. Finally, the juice was stored in a small jar with a tight-fitting lid. Not only did the students make colorful inks to use, they also made invisible and glow-in-the dark inks.

Number the phrases below in the order given in the story.

_____ **The mixture was stirred.**

_____ **Using the back of a wooden spoon, the berries were crushed.**

_____ **The ink was stored in a small jar with a tight-fitting lid.**

_____ **Berries were gathered.**

_____ **All the berry juice was strained into the bowl.**

_____ **The strainer was held over a bowl.**

_____ **Salt and vinegar were added to the berry juice.**

_____ **A strainer was filled with berries.**

 Look in a cookbook for a recipe you would like to try. Read all the steps. Have someone help you make the recipe. Be sure to follow each step in order.

Simon Says

 *When **following directions**, it is important to read the directions carefully and to follow them in the order they are listed.*

When you play Simon Says, you only follow the directions that Simon says. You do not follow any other directions. Play the game following the directions below.

1. Simon says draw a hand in the box below.

2. Simon says draw a ring on the ring finger.

3. Simon says draw fingernails on each finger.

4. Color each fingernail red.

5. Simon says write the names of five school days, one on each finger.

6. Circle your favorite day.

7. Write your teacher's name in the lower left-hand corner of the box.

8. Simon says write an addition problem on the hand, using the numbers 4, 5, and 9.

9. Now write a subtraction problem next to it.

10. Simon says draw a red scratch on the pinky finger.

11. Simon says draw a watch on the wrist.

12. Make the watch show 2:30.

13. Simon says outline the box with a yellow crayon.

14. Simon says write your name in the top right-hand corner of the box.

Sneaky Snakes

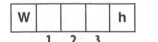

Snakes are very good at hiding. Most snakes can **camouflage** themselves into their environment. That means they have different colors and patterns on their bodies that allow them to blend in with the colors and patterns of things around them. Camouflage helps them hide from their enemies and helps them be **sneaky** when they are trying to capture something to eat. For example, the emerald tree boa lives in the **jungle**. Its green skin makes it nearly invisible among the green leaves of the trees. **Rattlesnakes** live in rocky, dry places. The patterns of black, tan, and brown on their backs help them blend in with their rocky environment. The horned viper lives in the desert. Its skin is the same color as **sand** where it burrows underground. It is hard to see unless it is moving. Also, some snakes that are harmless look very similar to **venomous** snakes. The harmless milk snake is colored orange, with yellow and black stripes, much like the poisonous **coral snake**. The enemies of the milk snake mistake it for a coral snake because they look so much alike.

Find the answers in the story. Write them in the puzzle.

1. Write the word that starts with a *v* and means "poisonous."

2. Write another word for "tricky."

3. Write what helps a snake blend in with its surroundings.

4. Write where emerald tree boas live.

5. Write what snakes live in rocky places and have black, tan, and brown patterned skin.

6. Write what is the same color as the horned viper.

7. Write the name of the snake that looks like a milk snake.

Write the letter from the numbered squares in the puzzle above to fill in each box.

| W | | | h | | | | | | | | | | | | | | | | | | | ! |
| 1 | 2 | 3 | | 4 | 5 | 6 | 7 | 8 | 9 | 10 | 11 | 12 | 13 | 14 | 15 | | 16 | 17 | 18 | 19 | 20 | 21 |

Fun With Words

Follow the directions to play each word game.

1. A palindrome is a word that is spelled the same forward or backward. Write each word backward. Circle each word that is a palindrome. Put an X on each word that is not.

wow _____

dad _____

mom _____

funny _____

noon _____

tall _____

deed _____

2. Some words imitate the noise that they stand for. For example, when you say "pop," it sounds like a popping sound! That is called onomatopoeia. Unscramble each noise word. Write it correctly.

seechrc _____

owp _____

plurs _____

mobo _____

lckic _____

zzisel _____

chnucr _____

3. Homophones are words that sound alike when you say them but are spelled differently and have different meanings. For example, see and sea are homophones. Draw a line to match each pair of homophones.

knot	flew
break	soar
flu	not
sore	write
right	road
rode	brake

4. Add or subtract letters from each word to change it into another word. Write the new word.

peach – ch + r = _____

shirt – irt + oe = _____

sports – p – rts + ccer = _____

love – ove + ike = _____

stove – st + n = _____

chicken – c – ick = _____

brother – bro + nei = _____

 Some names sound funny when you pronounce them backward. For example, Carol would be pronounced Lorac, and Jason would be pronounced Nosaj! Write your name and each of your classmates' names backward. Then pronounce each name. Are any of the names palindromes?

Where Is Holly?

 Drawing conclusions *means to make reasonable conclusions about events in a story using the information given.*

One day, while Mom was washing dishes in the kitchen, she realized that she had not heard a peep out of three-year-old Holly in a long time. The last time she had seen her, she was playing in the living room with some building blocks. "She sure is being good," thought Mom.

Write an X next to the best answer.

1. **Why did Mom think Holly was being good?**

   _____ Holly was washing dishes for her.

   _____ Holly was playing with dolls.

   _____ Holly was being so quiet.

After rinsing the last dish, Mom went to the living room to see what Holly had built. But Holly was not there. "Holly! Where are you?" Mom asked. Mom heard a faraway voice say, "Mommy!" So Mom went outside to see if Holly was there.

2. **Why did Mom go outside to look for Holly?**

   _____ Holly's voice sounded so far away.

   _____ The last time Mom saw Holly, she was riding her tricycle.

   _____ Holly said, "I'm outside, Mommy."

Mom looked down the street, up in the tree, and in the backyard, but Holly was not outside. She called her again but did not hear her voice. So, she went back inside. "Holly! Where are you? Come out right now."

3. **Why did Mom say, "Come out right now."**

   _____ She was mean.

   _____ She heard Holly's voice coming from the closet.

   _____ She thought Holly might be hiding.

Once again, Mom heard a faraway sound. "Help me!" cried Holly. Mom ran to the bathroom, but Holly was not there. She ran to the garage, but Holly was not there either. Finally, she ran to Holly's room and saw Holly's feet sticking out of the toy box, kicking wildly in the air!

4.   What had happened to Holly?

_____ She had fallen headfirst into the toy box and could not get out.

_____ She was playing with the blocks again.

_____ She was playing hide-and-seek with Mom.

Mom lifted Holly out of the toy box and asked, "Holly, are you all right?" Holly replied, "I think so."Holly then told Mom that she had been looking for her toy piano because she wanted to play a song for her. "Do you want to hear the song now?" Holly asked. "First, let's have a special snack. You can play the piano for me later," Mom suggested. Holly thought that was a great idea!

5.   Where was Holly's toy piano?

_____ The piano was under Holly's bed.

_____ The piano was at the bottom of the toy box.

_____ She was playing hide-and-seek with Mom.

Mom and Holly walked to the kitchen. Mom made Holly a bowl of ice cream with chocolate sauce and a cherry on top. Holly told Mom that she wanted to go to the park. Mom really liked that idea.

5.   What will Mom and Holly do next?

_____ Mom and Holly will go shopping.

_____ Mom and Holly will go for a bike ride.

_____ Mom and Holly will play on the swings in the park.

Read a chapter from a book. On another sheet of paper, write a sentence telling what you think will happen next. Read the next chapter. Were you correct?

Who Invented Potato Chips?

Have you ever wondered who invented the potato chip? Some people say George Crum was the first person to make them . . . by accident. In 1853, he was a chef at an elegant restaurant in Saratoga Springs, New York, called Moon's Lake House. A regular item on the menu was fried potatoes, which was an idea that had started in France. At that time, French fried potatoes were cut into thick slices. One day, a dinner guest at Moon's Lake House sent his fried potatoes back to the chef because he did not like them so thick. So, Mr. Crum cut the potatoes a little thinner and fried them. The guest did not like those either. That made Mr. Crum angry, so he thought he would just show that guy. He sliced the potatoes paper-thin and fried them, thinking that would hush the complaining diner. However, his plan backfired on him! The diner loved the crispy, thin potatoes! Other diners tried them and also liked them. So, Mr. Crum's potato chips were added to the menu. They were called Saratoga Chips. Eventually, Mr. Crum opened his own restaurant to sell his famous chips. Now potato chips are packaged and sold in grocery stores worldwide!

Color each chip and its matching bag the same color.

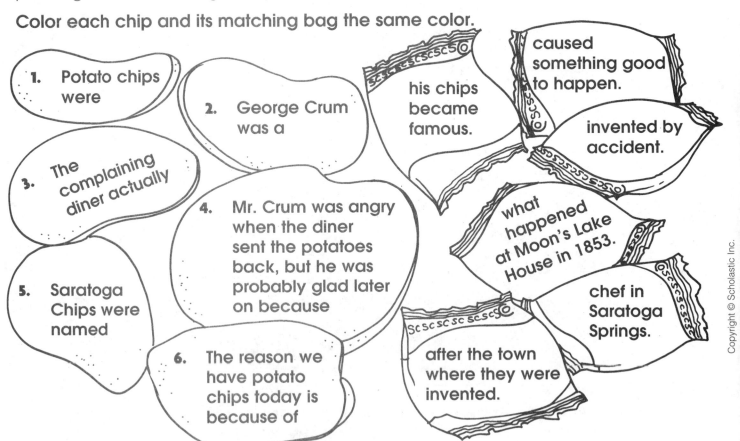

1. Potato chips were

2. George Crum was a

3. The complaining diner actually

4. Mr. Crum was angry when the diner sent the potatoes back, but he was probably glad later on because

5. Saratoga Chips were named

6. The reason we have potato chips today is because of

his chips became famous.

caused something good to happen.

invented by accident.

what happened at Moon's Lake House in 1853.

chef in Saratoga Springs.

after the town where they were invented.

The Lake Cabin

As you read the paragraph, imagine the scene that the words are describing. In the picture below, draw everything that has been left out. Color the picture.

My favorite thing to do in the summer is to go to Grandpa's lake cabin. In the evening after a full day of fishing, Grandpa and I sit on the back porch and enjoy the scenery. The sun setting behind the mountain fills the blue sky with streaks of orange and yellow. Colorful sailboats float by us in slow motion. Suddenly a fish jumps out of the water, making tiny waves in rings. A deer quietly walks to the edge of the water to get a drink. Red and yellow wildflowers grow near the big rock. On the shore across the lake, we see a couple of tents. Someone must be camping there. A flock of geese fly over the lake in the shape of a V. Every time we sit and look at the lake, Grandpa says, "This is the best place on earth!"

 On another sheet of paper, write a paragraph describing the place that you think is "the best place on earth." Read your paragraph to a friend.

Monroe's Mighty Youth Tonic

Way back yonder in 1853, a traveling salesman named "Shifty" Sam Monroe rode into our little town of Dry Gulch. I was there that day when Shifty stood on the steps of his **buckboard** selling Monroe's Mighty Youth Tonic. Shifty announced, "Ladies and gentlemen, **lend me your ears**. I, Sam Monroe, have invented a tonic that will give you back your youth. It will **put a spring in your step**. You'll feel years younger if you take a spoonful of this **heavenly elixir** once a day. It contains a **special blend of secret ingredients**. Why, it once made a 94-year-old cowboy feel so young, he went back to **bustin' broncs** again! An old settler that was over 100 felt so young he let out a **war whoop** that could be heard in Pike County! **It's a steal** at only one dollar a bottle. Step right up and get yours now." Well, I wondered what those secret ingredients were, so I bought a bottle and tasted it. It tasted like nothing but sugar water. So I hid behind Shifty Sam's wagon and waited for the crowd to **mosey** on home. When Shifty went inside to make some more tonic, I **kept my eye on him**. Sure enough, he mixed sugar and water and added a drop of vanilla. We'd been **hornswoggled**! I **hightailed it** right then over to the sheriff's office and had him arrest that no-good varmint. Old Shifty is now spending the rest of his "mighty youth" **behind bars**!

Howdy, partner! Read the bolded words in the story. What do they mean? Draw a rope to hitch up the words on the left with the correct meanings on the right.

1.	way back yonder	walk slowly
2.	buckboard	cheated; tricked
3.	Lend me your ears.	watched him closely
4.	Put a spring in your step.	making wild horses gentle
5.	heavenly elixir	ran quickly
6.	special blend of secret ingredients	evil creature
7.	bustin' broncs	Listen to me.
8.	war whoop	in jail
9.	It's a steal!	wagon
10.	mosey	You are getting it for a low price.
11.	kept my eye on him	I won't tell what's in it.
12.	hornswoggled	makes you feel peppy
13.	hightailed it	many years ago
14.	no-good varmint	loud yell
15.	behind bars	wonderful tonic

Double It Up

 *Some words can share the same spelling but have completely different meanings. To figure out the correct meaning of each word, use context clues. Using **context clues** means to look at the meaning of the whole sentence. One meaning for the word will make sense, and the other one will not. Read the following examples:*

The bat flew out of the dark cave. *(Would a baseball bat fly out of a cave? No. Then it must be the other kind of bat: a small flying animal.)*

He swung the bat so hard that the ball went over the fence. *(Would someone swing a small animal in order to hit a ball? Of course not!)*

Picture each of the following sentences in your mind to help you decide which meaning is correct for each italicized word. Then fill in the bubble next to the correct meaning.

1. I am sneezing because I have a *cold*.
  ○ opposite of hot
  ○ an illness

2. I rowed up to the *bank* and got out of the boat.
  ○ building where money is kept
  ○ shoreline of a river or creek

3. The garage is 15-*feet* wide.
  ○ a measurement
  ○ body parts used for walking

4. The *mouse* ran under the bushes.
  ○ a small, furry animal
  ○ hand control for a computer

5. I like to put butter on my *roll*.
  ○ bread
  ○ to turn over and over

6. Let's give the winner a big *hand*!
  ○ body part with fingers on it
  ○ applause

7. I *can* sing soprano.
  ○ a metal container
  ○ am able to

8. The wolf crept into the sheep *pen*.
  ○ writing instrument that uses ink
  ○ area that is fenced in

 On another sheet of paper, write two sentences showing a different meaning for the word "star" in each.

Where Am I?

 Making inferences *means to use information in a story to make judgments about information not given in the story.*

Read each riddle below. Look for clues to help you answer each question.

1. It is dark in here. I hear bats flying. With my flashlight, I see stalactites hanging above me. I hear water dripping. Where am I?

   _____

2. Let's sit in the front row! Ha ha ha! That's funny . . . a cartoon about a drink cup that is singing to a candy bar. That makes me hungry. I think I'll go get some popcorn before it starts. Where am I?

   _____

3. This thing keeps going faster and faster, up and down, and over and around. It tickles my tummy. The girls behind me are screaming. I hope I don't go flying out of my seat! Where am I?

   _____

4. I can see rivers and highways that look like tiny ribbons. I am glad I got to sit by the window. Wow, we are in a cloud! Yes, ma'am. I would like a drink. Thank you. Where am I?

   _____

5. I am all dressed up, sitting here quietly with my parents. The flowers are pretty. The music is starting. Here she comes down the aisle. I wish they would hurry so I can have some cake! Where am I?

   _____

6. Doctor, can you help my dog? His name is Champ. He was bitten by a snake, and his leg is swollen. I hope he will be all right. Where am I?

   _____

7. How will I ever decide? Look at all the different kinds. There are red hots, chocolates, candy corn, gummy worms, jawbreakers, and lollipops. Boy, this is my favorite place in the mall! Where am I?

   _____

8. This row has carrots growing, and this one has onions. The corn is getting tall. The soil feels dry. I better water the plants today. Don't you think so, Mr. Scarecrow? Where am I?

   _____

 On another sheet of paper, write two "Where Am I?" riddles of your own. Read your riddles to someone else and have them guess where you are.

Name _____

On the Border

 Classifying *means to put things into groups. One way to classify is to look for similarities, or ways things are alike.*

Read the words around the border of the picture. Find the words that belong with each picture. Write the words inside the picture. There will be five words in each picture.

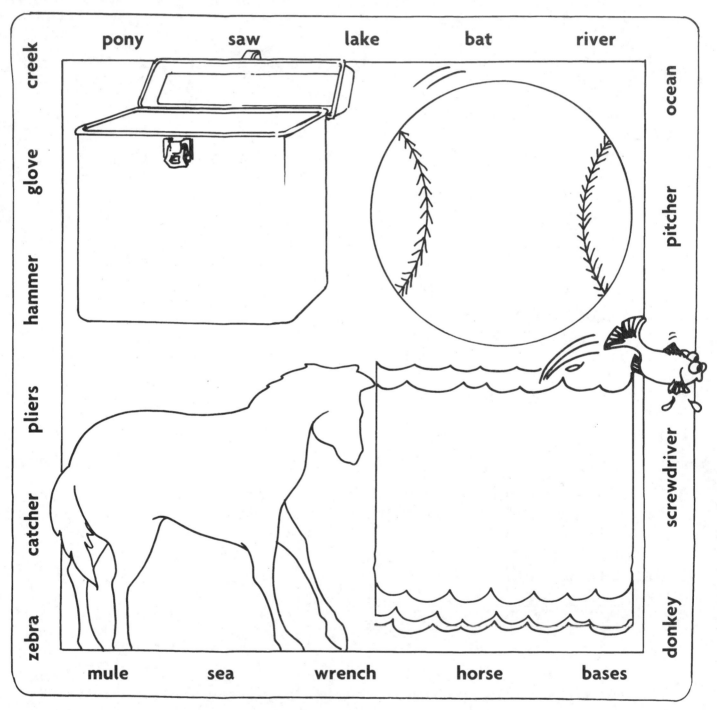

creek pony saw lake bat river ocean

glove

hammer pitcher

pliers

catcher screwdriver

zebra donkey

mule sea wrench horse bases

Moving In

The day we moved to our new house, there was a lot of work to do. Mom gave me the job of organizing the cabinets and closets. I unpacked each box and put things in their proper places. I filled up the medicine chest in the bathroom and the linen closet in the hall. I organized the silverware drawer in the kitchen, as well as the food in the pantry. I lined up Dad's stuff on the garage shelves. Last of all, I filled the bookshelf.

Write each word from the box in the correct category.

Medicine Chest	Linen Closet
_____	_____
_____	_____
_____	_____

Silverware Drawer	Pantry
_____	_____
_____	_____
_____	_____

Garage Shelves	Bookshelf
_____	_____
_____	_____
_____	_____

encyclopedias
eyedrops   teaspoons
car wax   motor oil
quilts   dictionary
cake mix   forks
serving spoons
atlas   aspirin
bandages   blankets
fishing tackle
crackers   novels
pillowcases
cereal   knives
sheets   toolbox
cough syrup
canned soup

THIS END UP

On another sheet of paper, make a list of eight things that people might store in an attic.

The Pyramid Game

Every morning before school, Mrs. Cavazos writes five words inside a pyramid on the chalkboard. When class begins, her students are to think of a title for the group of words. The title is to tell how the words are alike. The class then thinks of three words to add to the list.

Write a title for each pyramid of words.

Italian
French
English
Spanish
German

1. _____

fire
heaters
ovens
lava
electric blankets

2. _____

mouse
monitor
speakers
software
keyboard

3. _____

drums
flutes
tubas
trumpets
saxophones

4. _____

oaks
maples
pines
aspens
redwoods

5. _____

Easter
Hanukkah
Halloween
Fourth of July
Thanksgiving

6. _____

jets
blimps
airplanes
helicopters
hot air balloons

7. _____

nurse
doctor
lawyer
teacher
secretary

8. _____

roses
daisies
tulips
pansies
daffodils

9. _____

News or Views?

Facts *are true statement and can be proven.* **Opinions** *are a person's own personal views or beliefs.*

When people talk about things, they often mix news with opinions. Read each cartoon. Write *News* in the box if it is a fact. Write *Views* in the box If It Is a person's own personal opinion.

1. Punky Starr is the best rock singer that ever lived!

2. I like our new president. I think he is intelligent and kind.

3. Oranges were 3 for $1.00 at the Farmer's Market today.

4. Nobody likes me. Everyone thinks I am ugly.

5. When it gets dark, we will be able to see the Big Dipper and the North Star.

6. The city council will meet on Monday to vote on the new highway.

7. Ha ha ha ha! This show is funny.

8. The math homework for today is on page 34.

HOMEI PAGE

9. Your messy room looks like a pigpen!

TV Commercials

When you watch TV, you see a lot of commercials advertising different products. The people making the commercial want you to buy their product, so they make it sound as good as possible. Some of the things they say are facts, which can be proven. Other things are just the advertiser's opinion about how good the product is or how it will make you feel. Read each advertisement below. Write an *F* in the box beside each fact and an *O* in the box beside each opinion. The first one is done for you.

Eat at Billy Bob's Burgers.

[O] best burgers in town

[F] made with 100% beef

Drive an XJ-80 Sports Car today.

[ ] You'll never want to drive your old car again.

[ ] available in black, red, and silver

You'll be the Coolest Kid on Your Block with a Pair of Xtreme In-Line Skates!

[ ]

[ ] on sale for $79.99

Sky-Diving Adventure Video Game

[ ] joystick sold separately

[ ] You'll have hours and hours of fun!

Elastic Man, the Movie

[ ] full of heart-stopping action and mind-blowing special effects

[ ] "this year's best motion picture"

[ ] starring Academy-Award Winning Actor, Stretch Hamstring

[ ] now showing at the new Movie Town Theater

[ ] rated PG

 On another sheet of paper, design an ad for the Super Squirt Water Gun. Include two facts and two opinions.

News Report

Read the following news report about a tornado that touched down in a small town in Oklahoma. If the sentence is a fact that can be proven, underline it in red. If the sentence is someone's opinion, highlight it in yellow.

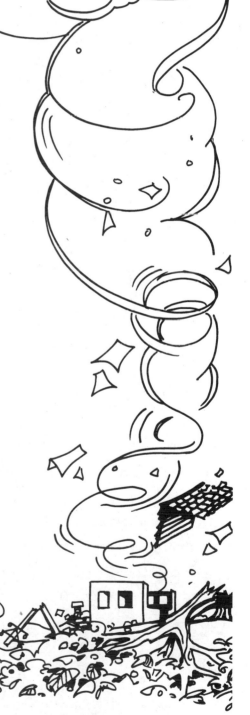

1. At 10:35 A.M. today, a tornado touched down briefly in the small town of Parksville, Oklahoma.

2. The roofs of several buildings were torn off by the strong winds.

3. Many large trees were uprooted.

4. There were no injuries.

5. "It was so loud, I thought a freight train was coming right through my living room!" Mrs. Cox exclaimed.

6. The National Weather Service issued a warning ten minutes before the tornado hit.

7. "I was afraid my house was going to blow away!" Mr. Carey reported.

8. Officer Reeves commented, "This may have been the worst day in the history of Parksville."

9. Electrical power was out for over two hours.

10. The large scoreboard at the football field was blown down.

11. "It will take forever to clean up this mess!" remarked Mrs. McDonald.

12. "I'm sure I can count on the people of Parksville to work together to rebuild our town," Mayor Clark said.

13. Donations to the rebuilding fund can be left at the bank.

 Write a news report about a tiger that escaped from the zoo. Include three facts and three opinions.

Name _____

Homer's Big Adventure

 Use details from a story to help determine what will happen next. This is called **making predictions**.

Brian was in such a hurry to get to the school bus on time that he forgot to close the door on Homer's cage after he fed him. Homer T. Hamster knew this was his big chance. He crawled out of his cage and ran downstairs, careful to sneak past Brian's mother without being seen. He ducked through a hole in the screen door and stepped out into the great backyard.

"Yippeeee!" cried Homer, throwing his little arms into the air. "I'm free at last!" He zipped through the gate and down the alley. The first thing Homer saw was a huge, snarling German shepherd who thought it was fun to chase anything that could run. "R-r-ruff! R-r-ruff!" Homer scurried here and there only inches ahead of the dog. He barely escaped by hiding under a flowerpot. "Whew, that was close!" he thought. He waited there awhile, shaking like a leaf.

Then he crept out into the alley again. He looked this way and that. The coast was clear, so he skipped happily along. He looked up just in time to see the big black tires of a pickup truck that was backing out of a driveway. He almost got squooshed! So, he darted quickly into someone's backyard where a boy was mowing the lawn. R-r-r-r-r! Homer had to jump out of the way again.

Back in the alley, he decided to rest somewhere that was safe. He crawled into a garbage dumpster and fell asleep. Later, he heard the sound of a big truck. He felt himself going high up into the air. The dumpster turned upside down, and the lid opened. Homer was falling. "Yikes!" screamed Homer. He had to think fast. He reached out and grabbed the side of the truck, holding on for dear life.

The truck rolled down the alley and into the street. As it turned the corner, Homer was flung off the truck and onto the hood of a school bus. He grabbed onto the windshield wipers as the bus drove to the corner and stopped.

The bus driver exclaimed, "Look, kids! There is a hamster riding on our bus!" All the kids rushed forward to see the funny sight. Homer looked through the windshield at all the surprised faces. All of a sudden, Homer saw Brian! Brian ran out of the bus and carefully picked up Homer. "Hey, buddy, how did you get out here? Are you okay?" Brian asked as he petted Homer's fur.

1. **What do you think happened next? Color the picture that seems to be the most likely ending to the story.**

2. **Underline the sentence that tells the main idea of the story.**

   Homer hid under a flowerpot to escape from a German shepherd.

   Homer had many exciting adventures after crawling out of his cage.

   Brian was surprised to see Homer riding the school bus.

3. **Do you think Homer will leave his cage again? Write a sentence to tell**

   why or why not._____

   _____

 On another sheet of paper, write a paragraph telling about one more adventure Homer might have had while he was out of his cage. Read your paragraph to a friend.

Mary's Mystery

Monday afternoon, Mom called my sister, Mary, to the door. The florist had just delivered a dozen red roses to her. "For me?" asked Mary. "Who would be sending me flowers?" Mom told her to read the card. It said, "Mary, I'm sorry I hurt your feelings. Can you forgive me?" Mary looked puzzled. She could not think of anyone that had hurt her feelings.

On Wednesday, a delivery boy brought a package to the door. He said, "This is for Mary." It was a box of chocolate candy. Mary liked chocolate very much, but she could not figure out who was sending her gifts, or why.

On Friday, a teenage girl dressed in a sparkly costume rang the doorbell. Mary answered the door. The teenager asked, "Are you Mary?" She nodded her head and said yes, and the teenager told her that she was sent by someone to perform a singing telegram. She sang, "Mary, I want you to be . . . the girl who will marry me . . ." Then she left. Mary looked at Mom. "I am only nine years old! I don't want to get married!" Mom laughed. "There must be some mistake."

That night, a handsome young man came to the door with a ring box in his hand. He rang the doorbell at Mary's apartment. Mary opened the door. When the man saw Mary, he looked surprised. He said, "Oh, I'm sorry. I was looking for Mary's apartment." Mary said, "Well, I am Mary." The man stood there frowning for a moment. Then he started to laugh.

"No wonder my girlfriend has not mentioned the gifts I sent her. I bet they have all been coming here." Then he told Mary to step outside and look at the metal numbers over her apartment door. Mary's apartment was #620, but the 6 had come loose and had turned upside down. That made it look like #920. The man said, "I am sorry about the mix-up. My girlfriend, Mary, just moved into apartment #920. I think all the delivery people saw your #920 and stopped here, just like I did. I guess when they found out your name was Mary, they thought they had the right place." Mary laughed. "Now I understand," she said. "Oh, I am sorry, but I already ate the chocolates." The man replied, "That's okay." Then as he turned to walk away he added, "You can also keep the flowers." "Thank you," Mary said grinning, "but I am not going to marry you!"

1. Underline two sentences below that tell what might happen next. Mark an *X* on two sentences that tell about something that probably will not happen.

   The man found the other Mary, his girlfriend, and gave her the ring.

   The man sent Mary a bill because she ate the chocolates.

   Nine-year-old Mary sent the man a dozen roses.

   Mary's mom turned the 9 over to make a 6 again and nailed it tight so their apartment number would be correct.

2. Circle what the title of the song the singing telegram might have been.

   "Love Me Always"

   "Crossing the Mississippi"

   "The Champion Cheer"

3. What did the florist deliver to Mary? _____

4. Which gift do you think Mary liked the best? Why? _____

   _____

5. On what day did Mary receive the singing telegram? _____

6. Where is the setting of this story? _____

Special Charts

Comparing and **contrasting** means to show the similarities and differences of things. A Venn diagram is a chart made of overlapping circles that can be used to organize the similarities and differences. The overlapping parts of the circles show how things are similar. The other part of the circles show how things are different.

Joe, Kim, and Rob each got a lunch tray, went through the lunch line, and sat together to eat. These students all had the same lunch menu, but each one only ate what he or she liked. Joe ate chicken nuggets, green beans, applesauce, and carrots. Rob ate chicken nuggets, green beans, a roll, and corn. Kim ate chicken nuggets, a roll, applesauce, and salad.

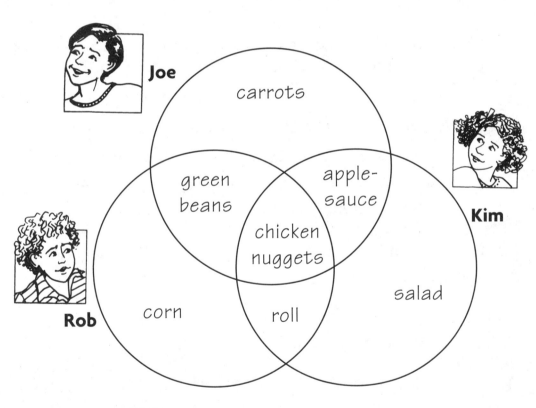

Today's Menu

chicken nuggets
corn
green beans
carrots
salad
roll
applesauce

1. What food did all three students eat? _____
2. What did Joe and Rob eat that Kim did not? _____
3. What did Joe and Kim eat that Rob did not? _____
4. What did Kim and Rob eat that Joe did not? _____
5. What did Joe eat that no one else ate? _____
6. What did Rob eat that no one else ate? _____
7. What did Kim eat that no one else ate? _____

Sports Chart

There are three brothers who love to play sports. Each one is good at several different sports. Jeff plays hockey, football, soccer, and baseball. Allen plays hockey, football, tennis, and golf. Seth plays hockey, tennis, soccer, and basketball.

1. Complete the Venn diagram showing which sports each brother plays. Start with the sport all three brothers have in common. Write it in the shared space of all three circles.

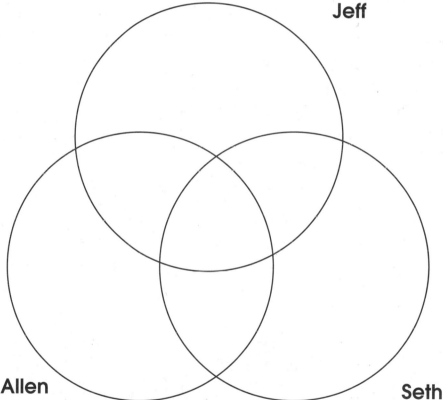

1. What sport do all three boys like to play? _____
2. What sport do Jeff and Allen like to play that Seth does not? _____
3. What sport do Jeff and Seth like to play that Allen does not? _____
4. What sport do Allen and Seth like to play that Jeff does not? _____
5. What sport does Jeff like to play that no one else does? _____
6. What sport does Allen like to play that no one else does? _____
7. What sport does Seth like to play that no one else does? _____

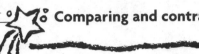

Sharks

There are over 400 different kinds of sharks. The whale shark is the largest. It is as big as a whale. The dwarf lantern is the smallest. It is only about seven inches long.

All sharks live in the ocean, which is salt water, but a few kinds can swim from salt water to fresh water. Bull sharks have been found in the Mississippi River!

Sharks do not have bones. They have skeletons made of cartilage, which is the same thing your ears and nose are made of. A shark's skin is made of spiky, hard scales. The jaws of a shark are the most powerful on earth. When a great white shark bites, it clamps down on its prey and thrashes its head from side to side. It is the deadliest shark.

Sharks eat fish, dolphins, and seals. The tiger shark will eat just about anything. Some fishermen have discovered unopened cans of food, clocks, boat cushions, and even a keg of nails inside tiger sharks. Sometimes sharks even eat other sharks. For example, a tiger shark might eat a bull shark. The bull shark might have eaten a blacktip shark. The blacktip shark might have eaten a dogfish shark. So a tiger shark could be found with three sharks in its stomach!

Some sharks look very unusual. The hammerhead shark has a head shaped somewhat like a hammer, with eyes set very far apart. A cookie cutter shark has a circular set of teeth. When it bites a dolphin or whale, it leaves a perfectly round hole in its victim. The sawshark has a snout with sharp teeth on the outside, which makes it look like a saw. The goblin shark has a sharp-pointed spear coming out of its head, and its ragged teeth make it look scary!

The mako shark is the fastest swimmer. Sometimes makos have been known to leap out of the water, right into a boat! These are just a few of the many kinds of fascinating sharks.

Name _____

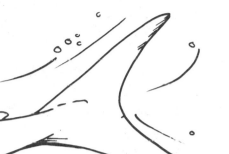

Complete the chart with the name of the correct shark. If the statement is about all sharks, write *all*.

1. the largest shark	whale shark
2. the smallest shark	
3. the deadliest shark	
4. the fastest swimmer	
5. live in the ocean	
6. have skeletons of cartilage	
7. has a sharp-pointed spear coming out of its head	
8. has a head shaped like a hammer	
9. skin of spiky, hard scales	
10. leaves a round bite mark	
11. looks like a saw	
12. has eaten unopened cans, clocks, and boat cushions	

 Read more about two different kinds of sharks. On another sheet of paper, list two similarities and two differences.

Earthquake!

*The **cause** in a story is what made something happen. The **effect** is what happened.*

Earthquakes are one of the most powerful events on the earth. When large sections of underground rock break and move suddenly, an earthquake occurs. This causes the ground to shake back and forth. Small earthquakes do not cause much damage, but large ones do. Some earthquakes have caused buildings and bridges to fall. Others have caused rivers to change their paths. Earthquakes near mountains and cliffs can cause landslides that cover up the houses and roads below. If a large earthquake occurs under the ocean, it can cause giant waves which flood the seashore. When large earthquakes occur in a city, there is danger of fire from broken gas lines and electric lines. Broken telephone lines and damaged roads make it difficult for rescue workers to help people who are in need. Scientists are trying to find ways to predict when an earthquake will happen so that people can be warned ahead of time.

Draw a shaky line under each effect.

Earthquakes can cause . . .
1. landslides
2. tornadoes
3. fires from broken gas and electric lines
4. huge waves that flood the seashore
5. swarms of flies
6. buildings and bridges to fall
7. sunburns
8. rivers to change their paths
9. damaged roads
10. lightning

Read about tornadoes. On another sheet of paper, make a list of eight things a tornado might cause.

Copyright © Scholastic Inc.

Wacky Water Slides

Have you ever gone to a water park in the summertime? Some of the most popular attractions are the water slides. How do they work? Construction crews put together sections of large plastic and fiberglass tubes to form the slides. They can make the tubes go straight down or around and around. Either way, the tubes must have a starting point that is high off the ground. This is because water slides work by gravity. Gravity is the natural pull of the earth. It is the force that makes things fall to the ground. So, when a swimmer begins to slide from up high, gravity pulls the swimmer down the slide into the pool below. There is another thing that water slides need in order to work. Water, of course! Water parks have huge pumps that pump the water to the top of the slides. The rushing water runs down the slides, making them slippery. Then the fun begins. Slip! Slide! Splash!

Fill in the blanks on each water slide to explain how they work.
Find the answers in the pool below.

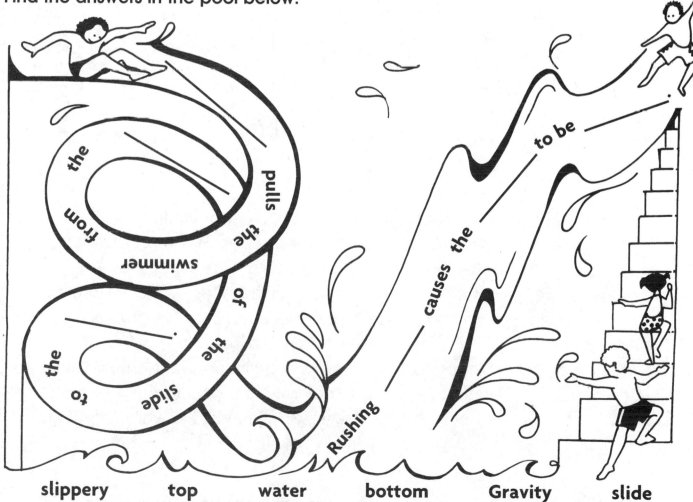

slippery   top   water   bottom   Gravity   slide

Nonfiction: A Biography

 A **biography** *is the history of a person's life. You have probably read biographies of presidents or famous people in history. The following biography is about one of the most popular zookeepers of our time.*

Steve Irwin

Steve Irwin was a famous TV personality and **reptile** specialist from **Australia**. People knew him as the **Crocodile Hunter**.

Steve's parents, Bob and Lyn Irwin, owned a reptile park. Steve grew up learning about and handling reptiles, as well as many other kinds of **animals**. When Steve was six years old, his father gave him a snake called a scrub **python**. Steve named it **Fred**. Steve's dad taught him all about the **wildlife** of Australia and took him on field trips to study about it. Steve often begged to go on these field trips rather than going to school. He caught his first crocodile when he was only nine years old.

Steve ran the Australia **Zoo**. He was a **herpetologist**. That means he was a reptile **expert**. His mission in life was to educate people about animals, teaching them to treat even dangerous animals with **respect**. Steve never hurt animals. In fact, he rescued many animals that were in **danger**, especially crocodiles. Steve was an expert snake handler. He always warned others, though, that picking up a **snake** is very dangerous.

Steve married an American who was visiting his zoo. Her name is **Terri**. Terri helped Steve handle the animals. They have one daughter. Her name is **Bindi**, and she loves animals, too. Steve Irwin died in 2006 while filming a TV show about dangerous animals.

Look at the bolded words in the story. Find each word in the puzzle and circle it. The words may go up, down, forward, backward, or diagonally.

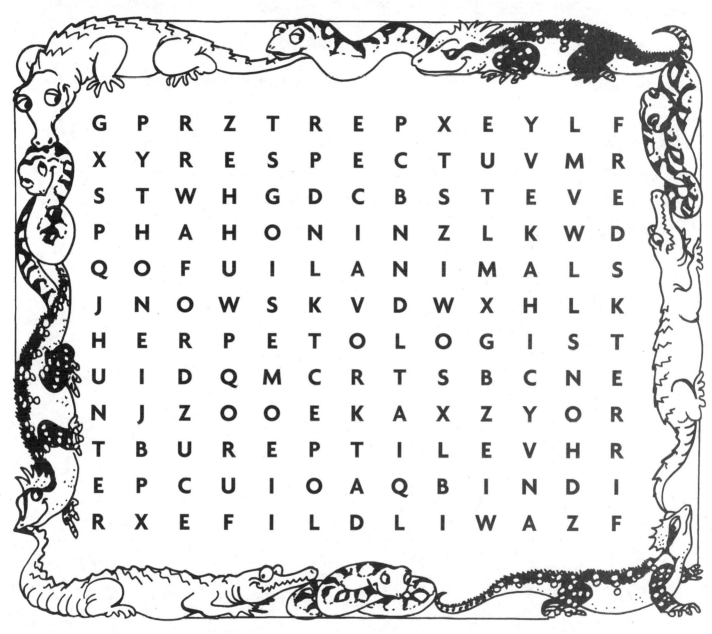

```
G  P  R  Z  T  R  E  P  X  E  Y  L  F
X  Y  R  E  S  P  E  C  T  U  V  M  R
S  T  W  H  G  D  C  B  S  T  E  V  E
P  H  A  H  O  N  I  N  Z  L  K  W  D
Q  O  F  U  I  L  A  N  I  M  A  L  S
J  N  O  W  S  K  V  D  W  X  H  L  K
H  E  R  P  E  T  O  L  O  G  I  S  T
U  I  D  Q  M  C  R  T  S  B  C  N  E
N  J  Z  O  O  E  K  A  X  Z  Y  O  R
T  B  U  R  E  P  T  I  L  E  V  H  R
E  P  C  U  I  O  A  Q  B  I  N  D  I
R  X  E  F  I  L  D  L  I  W  A  Z  F
```

List two facts about Steve Irwin.

1. _____

2. _____

 Find the biography section in the library. Check out a biography about someone who had a career that interests you.

Acrostic Poems

 Acrostic poetry is fun. An **acrostic poem** starts with a word that is the subject of the whole poem. The word is written vertically. Then words or phases about that subject are written using each letter. Look at the examples below.

Sleeping late
Under the ceiling fan
May we go to the pool?
My, it's hot!
Eating watermelon
Relaxing on vacation

Do you have a fever?
Open wide!
Checks for sore throat
Talks to the nurse
Orders some medicine
Ready for the next patient

Now it is your turn! Finish each acrostic poem below by writing something about the word that is written vertically, using each letter of the word.

T _____

Elementary school

A _____

C _____

Helps me learn

E _____

R _____

H _____

Oats for dinner

R _____

S _____

E _____

Saddle them up!

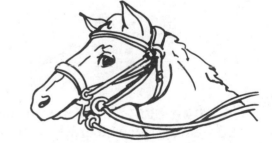

 On another sheet of paper, make an acrostic poem about yourself. Start by writing your name vertically.

Page 5
1. Alexander Graham Bell;
2. teacher of the deaf; 3. "Mr. Watson, come here! I want to see you!"; 4. Mr. Bell's assistant; 5. Bell demonstrated it to many people.

Page 6
Main Idea: The Milky Way is our galaxy.; Details: 1. stars; 2. outer; 3. spiral; 4. white; 5. sun; 6. billions

Page 7
Life on a wagon train was hard and dangerous.;1. oiling; 2. gathering; 3. cooking; 4. hauling; 5. hunting; 6. watching; 7. waiting; 8. crossing; 9. getting

Page 8
Main Idea: Elephants have very useful noses.; Sentences that do not belong: Some people like to ride on elephants.; Giraffes are the tallest animals in the world.; (The rest of the sentences are details.)

Page 9
The answer is 20.

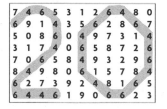

1. Mr. Jefferson, Riley, Rhonda; 2. C; 3. B; 4. Riley

Page 11
1. B; 2. E, A, D; 3. G; 4. F; 5. C, F

Page 12
1. land by the sea; 2. weather; 3. happens regularly; 4. outer covering of trees; 5. illness; 6. wood cut into boards; 7. no longer existing

Page 13

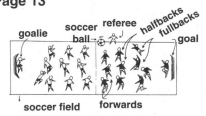

Page 14
A. 2, 1, 3; B. 1, 3, 2; C. 3, 2, 1; D. 2, 1, 3; E. 3, 1, 2; F. 3, 1, 2; G. 1, 3, 2; H. 2, 1, 3; I. 2, 1, 4, 3; J. 2, 4, 1, 3

Page 15
4, 6, 1, 3, 5, 2

Page 16
7, 4, 8, 1, 5, 3, 6, 2

Page 17
Check students' pages.

Page 18
1. venomous; 2. sneaky; 3. camouflage; 4. jungle; 5. rattlesnakes; 6. sand; 7. coral snake; Watch out for sneaky snakes!

Page 19
1. The palindromes are wow, dad, mom, noon, deed. (The other words are not.); 2. screech, pow, slurp, boom, click, sizzle, crunch; 3. knot–not; break–brake; flu–flew; sore–soar; right–write; rode–road; 4. pear, shoe, soccer, like, oven, hen, neither

Pages 20–21
1. Holly was being so quiet. 2. Holly's voice sounded so far away. 3. She thought Holly might be hiding. 4. She had fallen headfirst into the toy box and couldn't get out. 5. The piano was at the bottom of the toy box. 6. Mom and Holly will play on the swings in the park.

Page 22
1. Potato chips were invented by accident. 2. George Crum was a chef in Saratoga Springs. 3. The complaining diner actually caused something good to happen. 4. Mr. Crum was angry when the diner sent the potatoes back, but he was probably glad later on because his chips became famous. 5. Saratoga Chips were named after the town where they were invented. 6. The reason we have potato chips today is because of what happened at Moon's Lake House in 1853.

Page 23
Check students' drawings.

Page 25
1. way back yonder—many years ago; 2. buckboard—wagon; 3. Lend me your ears.—Listen to me.; 4. Put a spring in your step.—makes you feel peppy; 5. heavenly elixir—wonderful tonic; 6. special blend of secret ingredients—I won't tell what's in it.; 7. bustin' broncs—making wild horses gentle; 8. war whoop—loud yell; 9. It's a steal!—You are getting it for a low price.; 10. mosey—walk slowly; 11. kept my eye on him—watched him closely; 12. hornswoggled—cheated; tricked; 13. hightailed it—ran quickly; 14. no-good varmint—evil creature; 15. behind bars—in jail

Page 26
1. an illness; 2. shoreline of a river or creek; 3. a measurement; 4. a small, furry animal; 5. hot bread; 6. applause; 7. am able to; 8. area that is fenced in

Page 27
1. in a cave; 2. at a movie; 3. on a roller coaster; 4. on an airplane; 5. at a wedding; 6. at the vet; 7. at a candy store; 8. in a garden

Page 28
Toolbox: saw, screwdriver, wrench, pliers, hammer; Baseball: bat, pitcher, bases, catcher, glove; Horse: pony, donkey, horse, mule, zebra; Water: lake, river, ocean, sea, creek

Page 29
Medicine Chest: aspirin, cough syrup, bandages, eyedrops; Linen Closet: blankets, sheets; pillowcases, quilts; Silverware Drawer: forks, knives, teaspoons, serving spoons; Pantry: cereal, canned soup, crackers, cake mix; Garage Shelves: motor oil, toolbox, fishing tackle, car wax; Bookshelf: dictionary, novels, atlas, encyclopedias

Page 30

Wording of answers may vary:
1. Kinds of Languages; 2. Things That Are Hot; 3. Computer Equipment; 4. Musical Instruments; 5. Kinds of Trees; 6. Holidays; 7. Air Transportation; 8. Careers (or Occupations); 9. Kinds of Flowers

Page 31

1. views; 2. views; 3. news; 4. views; 5. news; 6. news; 7. views; 8. news; 9. views

Page 32

Burgers: O, F; Sports Car: O, F; In-line Skates: O, F; Video Game: F, O; Movie: O, O, F, F, F

Page 33

Facts: 1, 2, 3, 4, 6, 9, 10, 13
Opinions: 5, 7, 8, 11, 12

Page 35

1. Color the picture of Homer in his cage. 2. Homer had many exciting adventures after crawling out of his cage. 3. Answers will vary.

Page 37

1. Underline: The man found the other Mary, his girlfriend, and gave her the ring.; Mary's mom turned the 9 over to make a 6 again and nailed it tight so their apartment number would be correct.; Mark an *X* on: The man sent Mary a bill because she ate the chocolates.; Nine-year-old Mary sent the man a dozen roses.; 2. "Love Me Always"; 3. a dozen red roses; 4. Answers will vary.; 5. Friday; 6. Mary's apartment

Page 38

1. chicken nuggets; 2. green beans; 3. applesauce; 4. roll; 5. carrots; 6. corn; 7. salad

Page 39

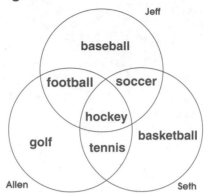

1. hockey; 2. football; 3. soccer; 4. tennis; 5. baseball; 6. golf; 7. basketball

Page 41

1. whale shark; 2. dwarf lantern; 3. great white shark; 4. mako shark; 5. all; 6. all; 7. goblin shark; 8. hammerhead shark; 9. all; 10. cookie cutter shark; 11. sawshark; 12. tiger shark

Page 42

1, 3, 4, 6, 8, 9

Page 43

Gravity pulls the swimmer from the **top** of the slide to the **bottom**.

Rushing **water** causes the **slide** to be **slippery**.

Page 45

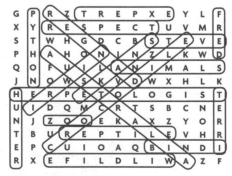

Facts will vary.

Page 46

Answers will vary.